Alberta D. Jones

BAHAMUT AND THE WAQWAQ TREE

GAME GUIDE

Strategies, Secrets, and Walkthroughs for Every Adventurer

Chapter 1. Introduction to Bahamut and the Waqwaq Tree..........5

    1.1 Overview of the Game World..5

    1.2 Storyline and Lore...10

    1.3 Key Features and Highlights..14

    1.4 Game Modes and Accessibility Options............................19

Chapter 2. Gameplay Mechanics..25

    2.1 Basic Controls and Navigation...25

    2.2 Combat System Explained...28

    2.3 Exploration and Environmental Interaction...................32

    2.4 Managing Resources and Inventory.................................36

Chapter 3. Character Classes and Roles..............................41

    3.1 Character Overview and Specializations.........................41

    3.2 Strengths and Weaknesses of Each Role.........................42

    3.3 Abilities and Skills for Different Playstyles....................44

    3.4 Customizing Your Character's Growth............................45

Chapter 4. Weapons and Equipment...................................47

    4.1 Types of Weapons and Their Functions..........................47

    4.2 Armor and Defensive Gear...48

    4.3 Item Crafting and Upgrades...49

    4.4 Managing Your Equipment for Success...........................50

Chapter 5. Strategies and Tips..53

    5.1 Early Game Tips for Beginners...53

    5.2 Combat Tactics and Boss Fight Strategies......................54

    5.3 Resource Management for Progression...........................56

    5.4 Navigating the Dangerous Waqwaq Tree........................57

Chapter 6. Walkthroughs for Missions and Levels............................59

6.1 Main Story Mission Walkthrough....................................59

6.2 Side Quests and Optional Objectives............................61

6.3 Strategies for Surviving the Waqwaq Tree's Challenges.62

6.4 Boss Fights and How to Conquer Them 63

Chapter 7. Secrets and Collectibles 66

7.1 Hidden Areas and Secret Locations 66

7.2 Collectibles and Their Role in the Story 68

7.3 Easter Eggs and Fun Discoveries 69

7.4 Unlockable Content and Special Rewards....................71

Chapter 8. Achievements and Trophies 73

8.1 Overview of Achievements and Trophies....................73

8.2 Tips for Earning All Achievements 74

8.3 Missable Achievements and How to Get Them..........76

8.4 Special Achievements for Completionists 78

Chapter 9. Advanced Techniques..80

9.1 Mastering Combat and Advanced Movement..............80

9.2 Optimizing Your Build and Playstyle 82

9.3 Speedrunning and Efficient Strategies........................84

9.4 Customizing the Game's Difficulty for Advanced Players86

Chapter 10. Additional Resources 88

10.1 Official Game Website and Forums 88

10.2 Community Resources and Fan Websites....................89

10.3 Modding Communities and Custom Content 91

10.4 Troubleshooting and Technical Support......................93

Chapter 1. Introduction to Bahamut and the Waqwaq Tree

1.1 Overview of the Game World

Bahamut and the Waqwaq Tree immerses players in a beautifully crafted world where ancient myths collide with the forces of nature, powerful creatures, and complex civilizations. The game world is a vibrant and living place, full of magical elements, mysterious forests, and monumental landscapes. Every corner of this universe is rich with lore, secrets, and opportunities for discovery. In this section, we'll take a deep dive into the world that players will explore, the factions and creatures they will encounter, and the elements that define the game's environment.

The Setting: A World on the Brink of Transformation

The game is set in the mythical land of **Samar**, a sprawling world filled with a rich tapestry of cultures, ecosystems, and conflicting powers. At its heart is the **Waqwaq Tree**, an ancient and sacred tree believed to hold the balance of nature and the fabric of life itself. Towering over the landscape, the Waqwaq Tree is both revered and feared, with rumors surrounding its power to either save or destroy the world. Its influence can be seen throughout the land, shaping the climate, flora, fauna, and the destinies of those who live nearby.

The world is divided into several distinct regions, each with its own environmental themes and cultures:

- **The Verdant Wilds**: A lush, expansive forest surrounding the Waqwaq Tree. The landscape is teeming with vibrant plant life, mystical creatures, and ancient ruins, many of which are remnants of the world's early civilizations. The region is full of secrets, including hidden paths that only those who understand the ancient language of the forest can navigate. Dangerous beasts, including spectral wolves and fire-breathing lizards, roam the forest, challenging adventurers at every turn.

- **The Arid Reaches**: Vast deserts and sand dunes stretch across the southern lands, where the climate is harsh and unforgiving. The Arid Reaches are home to nomadic tribes that have adapted to the environment, but even they fear the ancient creatures that slumber beneath the sand. The scorching sun and shifting dunes conceal treasures and lost artifacts from long-forgotten civilizations, but also dangerous sandstorms and deadly predators.

- **The Frostbound Peaks**: North of the Verdant Wilds, towering icy mountains rise high above the land. These snow-covered peaks are home to rugged clans of warriors who endure harsh winters and dangerous wildlife, including ice giants and mystical snow creatures. The Frostbound Peaks are rich in rare minerals and ancient magic, but only the brave or foolish venture here due to the relentless cold and the perilous terrain.

- **The Celestial Plains**: The plains stretch far beyond the horizon, a vast area where the sky and land seem to merge. Home to peaceful agricultural communities and the spiritual centers of the game's main factions, this region is often considered the heart of Samar. It's here that travelers meet the mystical sages and monks who seek the wisdom of the

Waqwaq Tree. It is rumored that the plains hold the key to unlocking the secrets of the universe.

- **The Sunken Depths**: An underwater world located beneath the surface of Samar. The Sunken Depths are a series of vast caverns and ancient cities submerged beneath the ocean. Here, remnants of an ancient aquatic civilization can be found, and the forgotten powers that lie within the deep waters could change the fate of the world. Adventurers who venture here face treacherous waters, hostile sea creatures, and the constant threat of drowning.

Magic and Mysticism

Magic is a central theme in the world of *Bahamut and the Waqwaq Tree*. The land is filled with powerful forces, from elemental magic to arcane rituals tied to the Waqwaq Tree itself. The Tree is said to be a source of immense power, controlling both life and death, and its very existence is tied to the balance of the world. Different regions draw on various forms of magic, and those who can harness it gain access to extraordinary abilities.

- **Elemental Magic**: The forces of nature are alive in Samar, with elemental magic governing fire, water, earth, and air. This magic allows players to manipulate the environment— creating paths in dangerous terrain, summoning powerful creatures, or using fire and ice to defeat enemies.

- **Life Magic**: The Waqwaq Tree's most significant influence is in the realm of life. Those who attune themselves to its power can heal, rejuvenate, and communicate with the world's plants and animals. This form of magic is vital to the game's storyline, as players seek to unlock the mysteries of the Tree and restore balance to the world.

- **Dark and Forbidden Magic**: In the darker corners of the world, there are those who dabble in forbidden arts. These practices are often tied to the destruction of the Waqwaq Tree and the corruption of nature itself. As players explore, they may encounter ruins and dungeons filled with dark magic, which can either be wielded as a weapon or used for destructive purposes.

Factions and Political Tensions

The game world is populated by numerous factions, each with its own goals, values, and desires for control over the Waqwaq Tree. The political landscape is a complex web of alliances, rivalries, and conflicts. Players will need to navigate these dynamics as they progress through the game, choosing which factions to support and which to oppose.

- **The Verdant Order**: A faction of druids and nature protectors who revere the Waqwaq Tree. They believe that the Tree is a divine being, and their mission is to preserve and protect its sanctity at all costs. Their magic is closely tied to the land and creatures, and they seek to maintain balance in the world by any means necessary.

- **The Empire of Seldor**: A powerful military empire located in the Celestial Plains. Seldor seeks to expand its reach and gain control of the Waqwaq Tree to harness its power for domination. The empire is technologically advanced, with an army equipped with the latest weapons and magical enhancements. They see the Tree as a tool to further their ambitions.

- **The Forgotten Ones**: A shadowy group that exists on the fringes of the world. They are followers of forbidden magic and wish to corrupt the Waqwaq Tree's power for themselves. They are a dangerous and mysterious faction, often working in secret to disrupt the balance of the world.

The Threat of Bahamut

At the heart of the game's conflict is the legendary creature **Bahamut**, an ancient being whose presence has been felt throughout the history of Samar. Once a protector of balance, Bahamut's fall from grace has thrown the world into turmoil. Its once noble heart has become consumed by darkness, and it now seeks to control the Waqwaq Tree's immense power for its own gain.

Bahamut's influence extends across the world, leaving corruption and chaos in its wake. As the protagonist, players must confront Bahamut's minions and uncover the truth behind its fall, all while dealing with the factions that seek control over the Tree's power.

Dynamic World Interactions

The world of *Bahamut and the Waqwaq Tree* reacts dynamically to the player's actions. Your decisions shape the environment, from altering the landscape to shifting the political climate. Certain areas may change depending on which factions you align with or whether you use magic to manipulate the environment. The world adapts to your journey, offering new challenges and rewards based on your choices.

1.2 Storyline and Lore

The storyline of *Bahamut and the Waqwaq Tree* is one of ancient prophecy, corruption, and the struggle for balance in a world teetering on the edge of destruction. Set in the mythical land of **Samar**, the game immerses players in a rich tapestry of history, lore, and an impending conflict between nature and the forces of darkness. Central to the narrative is the **Waqwaq Tree**, an ancient, mystical entity that serves as the heartbeat of the world.

The Beginning: The Age of Harmony

Long before the events of the game, Samar was a world of peace and prosperity. The **Waqwaq Tree** stood at the heart of this harmony, its roots extending deep into the earth, channeling the very essence of life itself. Its branches stretched toward the heavens, bringing balance between nature, magic, and the many civilizations that inhabited the world. The ancient civilizations that once flourished in Samar revered the Tree, believing it to be the embodiment of the natural forces that governed their world.

In the Age of Harmony, the forces of nature—earth, water, fire, and air—thrived in perfect equilibrium. Various factions, including the druids of the **Verdant Order** and the peaceful people of the **Celestial Plains**, lived in cooperation with the land, guided by the wisdom of the Waqwaq Tree. This unity allowed both magic and civilization to prosper, with the Tree's influence nourishing all life in Samar.

However, all was not perfect. Lurking in the shadows, there were factions that sought to exploit the Tree's power, believing that if they could control its life-giving energy, they would have the means to rule the world.

The Rise of Bahamut: The Fall from Grace

The rise of **Bahamut**, once a revered guardian spirit of the world, marked the beginning of Samar's downfall. Bahamut was originally a divine being, tasked with maintaining balance and ensuring the continued harmony of nature. His role was to protect the world from external threats and keep the forces of darkness at bay.

But over time, Bahamut grew disillusioned with his task. He saw the growing reliance on the Waqwaq Tree's power as a weakness. The once noble protector began to believe that the only way to save the world was to control the very source of life—the Waqwaq Tree. He believed that by absorbing its immense power, he could become the ultimate being, capable of enforcing his own vision of balance and order upon the world, a vision where he alone would hold the reins of creation and destruction.

Bahamut's ambition grew, and he secretly began to corrupt the Waqwaq Tree's sacred energy. Slowly, he transformed from a protector to a conqueror, consumed by a hunger for power. In his pursuit, he unleashed dark, destructive forces upon the world—an event that would later be known as **The Shattering**.

The Shattering: A World in Chaos

The Shattering marked the beginning of a catastrophic series of events that reshaped the very fabric of Samar. Bahamut's corruption of the Waqwaq Tree caused a massive rupture in the natural order. The Tree's life-giving magic became tainted, throwing the world into disarray. Regions that were once lush and fertile began to wither, while other areas, like the **Arid Reaches**, were overcome by storms and unnatural droughts. A wave of corruption spread across the land, warping creatures and creating monstrous abominations.

As Bahamut's influence grew, the Waqwaq Tree's protective aura began to fade, and those who depended on it for survival found themselves facing unprecedented challenges. Factions that once thrived in unity—like the **Verdant Order** and the peaceful communities of the **Celestial Plains**—found themselves in conflict. Distrust and fear spread among the factions as they competed for control of the Tree and its remaining power.

The age-old prophecy, the **Book of Waqwaq**, long thought to be a mere myth, was uncovered. It spoke of a time when the Waqwaq Tree would falter, and the world would require a hero to restore balance. This prophecy hinted at the rise of a champion who could either heal the Tree's corruption or see the world destroyed by Bahamut's will.

The Present: The Player's Role in the Story

As the protagonist of *Bahamut and the Waqwaq Tree*, you play a crucial role in the unfolding events. You are a descendant of an ancient line of warriors and scholars who were once entrusted with the care of the Waqwaq Tree. The story begins with your return to Samar after years of exile, having been raised away from the growing conflict. The land is now in turmoil, and your once peaceful homeland is now under the shadow of Bahamut's corruption.

Your journey begins when you receive a mysterious summons from the **Verdant Order**, who believe you are the one mentioned in the ancient prophecy—the one who can either restore the Waqwaq Tree or witness its destruction. As you venture across Samar, you will encounter various factions, some of whom will aid you, while others, like Bahamut's loyal followers, will work to thwart your efforts.

Along the way, you will uncover long-forgotten secrets of the past, learn the truth about Bahamut's fall from grace, and discover the ancient magic that binds the world together. The choices you make will determine the fate of Samar. Will you be able to cleanse the Waqwaq Tree's corruption and restore balance? Or will you succumb to Bahamut's influence and let the world fall into eternal darkness?

The Prophecy of the Waqwaq Tree

The **Prophecy of the Waqwaq Tree** plays a central role in the narrative. According to the prophecy, the Waqwaq Tree's life force is tied to the world itself. Should it die or be corrupted beyond repair, the very world will unravel. The prophecy suggests that only someone who understands both the ancient magic and the balance between light and darkness can heal the Tree. Yet, it also warns that the Tree's salvation comes at a great cost, as the forces of nature will demand a sacrifice in return for the restoration of harmony.

As you progress, you will encounter artifacts, ancient tomes, and cryptic messages that will guide you through your journey, but ultimately, the choices you make regarding the Waqwaq Tree's fate will be your own.

The Legacy of the Waqwaq Tree

The lore surrounding the Waqwaq Tree extends beyond its connection to Bahamut's fall. The Tree is said to be a living manifestation of the cosmos itself—its roots spreading into the earth, while its branches touch the stars. According to some ancient texts, the Tree is not only a source of life for Samar but is also tied to the very forces that govern time, space, and magic. Some even believe that the Waqwaq Tree is a doorway to other worlds, existing beyond the boundaries of the known universe.

As you explore Samar, you will learn that the Tree is not just a physical entity but also a symbol of the interconnectedness of all life. The balance between nature, magic, and civilization can only be maintained if the Waqwaq Tree continues to thrive. However, Bahamut's fall from grace has fractured that balance, and it's now up to you to decide whether the Tree will be saved or destroyed— and what that will mean for the future of the world.

1.3 Key Features and Highlights

Bahamut and the Waqwaq Tree is more than just a visually stunning fantasy RPG—it's a deeply immersive experience that blends storytelling, exploration, tactical combat, and character development into a unified adventure. Below are the key features and standout highlights that define the game and make it a must-play for fans of rich, lore-driven fantasy worlds and strategic gameplay.

A Living, Breathing World

One of the most remarkable aspects of *Bahamut and the Waqwaq Tree* is its fully dynamic and interactive game world. Samar is not static—it reacts to your choices, evolves as the story progresses, and offers different experiences based on your path. This immersive design brings the following elements to life:

- **Dynamic Ecosystems**: Forests grow or wither depending on your actions. Magic corruption can be reversed or spread, changing the layout and creatures of each region.

- **Environmental Storytelling**: Ancient ruins, crumbling cities, and magical anomalies tell their own stories through visuals, lore fragments, and environmental changes over time.

- **Day-Night Cycle and Weather Systems**: Time and weather affect enemy behavior, access to certain areas, and the effectiveness of magic or weapons.

Branching Narrative with Player-Driven Choices

The game features a rich and branching storyline where your decisions truly matter. Whether you ally with certain factions, use forbidden magic, or choose peace over conquest, your choices will impact both your character's journey and the fate of the world.

- **Multiple Endings**: Shape the destiny of Samar by guiding the outcome of the war between Bahamut and the Waqwaq Tree.

- **Faction Alliances**: Form alliances with one of the major factions—The Verdant Order, The Empire of Seldor, or even the mysterious Forgotten Ones—each with unique quests, storylines, and consequences.

- **Moral Dilemmas**: Many quests feature grey-area decisions that force players to weigh immediate benefits against long-term consequences.

Deep Combat and Magic Systems

Combat in *Bahamut and the Waqwaq Tree* is both strategic and fluid, blending traditional action RPG mechanics with real-time decision-making and tactical depth.

- **Multi-Class Combat System**: Mix and match skills from different class archetypes (such as Elementalist, Shadowblade, or Beastcaller) to create a hybrid playstyle.

- **Elemental Synergies**: Use the environment to your advantage. Cast fire spells on oil-covered fields, freeze rivers to cross them, or call down lightning during thunderstorms.

- **Enemy Adaptation AI**: Enemies learn from your fighting style and adapt over time, making repeat encounters feel fresh and challenging.

Expansive Customization and Progression

Tailor your character's build to suit your playstyle. The game provides a robust leveling and gear system, giving players control over how their hero evolves.

- **Skill Trees and Perks**: Each class has its own extensive skill tree, and cross-class perks can be unlocked based on exploration and quest progression.

- **Equipment and Crafting**: Discover rare materials throughout Samar and forge your own weapons, enchant gear, or upgrade armor to suit specific challenges.

- **Spirit Bonding**: Bind magical spirits from the Waqwaq Tree to your soul, granting new powers and passive abilities based on the spirits you choose.

Exploration and Secrets Abound

The world is densely packed with secrets, hidden locations, and mystical artifacts waiting to be uncovered.

- **Open-World Freedom**: Choose your path and explore the world at your own pace. Whether you're following the main quest or tracking down long-lost relics, exploration is always rewarded.

- **Puzzle Shrines and Trials**: Solve ancient environmental puzzles and complete timed challenges to gain access to rare abilities and lore insights.

- **Mythic Creatures**: Encounter and tame (or defeat) legendary beasts that protect sacred sites of the Waqwaq Tree.

Cinematic Presentation and Immersive Soundtrack

The game features stunning visuals and atmospheric music that deepen your emotional connection to the world and its characters.

- **High-Fidelity Visuals**: Hand-crafted environments and character designs inspired by mythologies from Southeast Asia and the Middle East.

- **Narrative Cutscenes**: Fully voice-acted cinematic scenes highlight key story moments and character development.

- **Dynamic Soundtrack**: Music adapts to your actions, with orchestral themes shifting from tranquil exploration to tense combat seamlessly.

Multiplayer and Social Integration (Optional)

While primarily a single-player experience, the game includes optional online and social features:

- **Co-op Trials**: Team up with friends for special co-op boss battles and dungeon runs that offer unique loot and prestige rewards.

- **Community Lore Challenges**: Participate in time-limited world events where players globally uncover hidden lore and shape upcoming seasonal content.

- **Photo Mode and Lore Journal Sharing**: Capture your journey and share in-game journal entries with the community.

Next-Gen Polish and Accessibility Options

Bahamut and the Waqwaq Tree is built for accessibility and performance:

- **Cross-Platform Play (Where Available)**: Seamlessly transition between PC and console versions.

- **Accessibility Features**: High-contrast UI, customizable controls, adaptive difficulty settings, and narrated menus ensure everyone can enjoy the game.

- **Performance Optimization**: Smooth frame rates and loading times even in vast open-world zones.

1.4 Game Modes and Accessibility Options

Bahamut and the Waqwaq Tree has been designed with inclusivity and replayability in mind, offering a variety of game modes and accessibility features that cater to a wide range of players—from casual adventurers to hardcore strategists. Whether you're here for the immersive story, tactical combat, exploration, or cooperative trials, the game ensures every player can tailor their experience to their personal preferences and needs.

Story Mode

Story Mode is ideal for players who are primarily interested in the narrative, world-building, and exploration aspects of the game.

- **Lower Combat Difficulty**: Enemies are less aggressive and deal less damage, allowing players to progress through the story at their own pace.

- **Focus on Lore and Character Development**: Additional dialogues and lore journals are more accessible, with prompts guiding players to rich story elements.

- **Auto-Puzzle Assistance**: Optional hints and visual markers help guide players through environmental puzzles or riddles related to the Waqwaq Tree.

This mode is especially suited for newcomers to RPGs, lore-lovers, and players with limited time for grinding or deep combat engagement.

Adventure Mode (Standard)

The default experience, **Adventure Mode**, provides a balanced blend of story, exploration, and tactical combat.

- **Standard Enemy Behavior**: Combat feels dynamic and moderately challenging, requiring attention to elemental interactions, skill usage, and enemy patterns.

- **Scalable Challenges**: Optional tougher dungeons and "Verdant Trials" are available for those looking to test their skills without increasing the overall game difficulty.

- **Exploration-Focused**: Hidden areas, collectibles, and side quests are subtly integrated for those who take time to explore off the beaten path.

Adventure Mode is recommended for most players, offering a satisfying challenge while maintaining full immersion in the story.

Elder Trial Mode (Hardcore)

Elder Trial Mode is designed for experienced players who seek intense strategic depth and high-stakes decision-making.

- **Enemy Adaptation AI Enabled**: Foes will learn from your tactics, dodge repeated strategies, and use countermeasures.

- **No Respawn Zones**: Some areas become permadeath zones—failure results in restarting the dungeon or losing temporary progress.

- **Environmental Hazards Intensified**: Corruption spreads faster, weather changes become more impactful (e.g., lightning storms empowering enemies), and magic anomalies become more frequent.

Rewards for completing quests and dungeons in Elder Trial Mode include exclusive armor sets, cosmetic rewards, and lore fragments that are inaccessible in other modes.

Cooperative & Online Challenges

Though primarily a single-player experience, *Bahamut and the Waqwaq Tree* features optional online modes that expand the scope of gameplay.

- **Co-op Trials**: Team up with friends or random players to tackle high-level dungeons or world bosses. Rewards scale based on teamwork efficiency and synergy.

- **Seasonal Lore Events**: Participate in limited-time, lore-based community quests where global progress shapes the game's world state for all players.

- **Warden's Arena (PvP)**: A controlled, lore-justified player-versus-player zone where elite players can test builds and tactics in 1v1 or team duels.

These online elements are opt-in, meaning players who prefer a purely solo experience can enjoy the full story and progression without participating in multiplayer.

Comprehensive Accessibility Options

The development team behind *Bahamut and the Waqwaq Tree* has placed a strong emphasis on inclusivity, ensuring that the game is accessible to as many players as possible through a robust suite of features:

Visual Accessibility

- **Colorblind Modes**: Presets for deuteranopia, protanopia, and tritanopia with optimized HUD color palettes.

- **High-Contrast UI**: Toggle options to increase text/background contrast for easier readability.

- **Font Scaling**: Adjustable font sizes for subtitles, menus, and dialogue.

Hearing Accessibility

- **Closed Captions**: Customizable captions that display environmental sounds, enemy alerts, and character tones.

- **Sound Substitution**: Vibration and visual indicators for key audio cues (e.g., stealth detection, spell charges).

Motor Accessibility

- **Fully Remappable Controls**: Customize controller or keyboard layouts to suit individual comfort and range of motion.

- **One-Hand Mode**: Simplified control presets for one-handed gameplay using macros and auto-targeting.

- **Toggle vs. Hold Options**: Switch between toggle or hold for key inputs (e.g., aiming, running, blocking).

Cognitive and Gameplay Assistance

- **Simplified Combat Mode**: Optional mode reduces input complexity, letting the game handle combos and elemental interactions for players who want to focus on positioning and decision-making.

- **Gameplay Speed Adjustment**: Slow down real-time action sequences for players who need more time to react and strategize.

- **Waypoint and Objective Tracking Aids**: Visual path tracing and customizable quest reminders help prevent disorientation or memory overload.

New Game+ and Replay Value

After completing the main storyline, players unlock **New Game+**, which offers:

- **Enhanced Difficulty Levels**

- **Retained Progression**: Carry over abilities, gear, and lore logs.

- **Alternate Choices and Endings**: Explore different branches of the story, unlock hidden character arcs, or ally with previously hostile factions.

New Game+ keeps *Bahamut and the Waqwaq Tree* engaging even after the credits roll, providing reasons to return to Samar time and again.

Chapter 2. Gameplay Mechanics

2.1 Basic Controls and Navigation

Understanding the core controls and navigation systems in *Bahamut and the Waqwaq Tree* is essential for new players and veterans alike. The game strikes a balance between intuitive exploration and tactical precision, offering responsive controls tailored for both controller and keyboard/mouse setups. This section outlines the basic movement, interaction, and interface mechanics that form the foundation of your journey through the mystical world of Samar.

Movement and Camera Controls

The movement system allows smooth traversal of diverse environments, from dense enchanted forests to ancient ruins and floating isles corrupted by magical anomalies.

- **Analog/Directional Movement**: Use the left stick (or WASD keys) to move your character. Movement speed adapts based on how far you push the stick or how long you hold a key.

- **Camera Control**: The right stick (or mouse) controls the camera angle. It's highly adjustable and can be locked during cinematic sequences or freely rotated during exploration.

- **Jumping and Climbing**: Tap the jump button to leap over obstacles or gaps. Certain surfaces can be scaled or clung to, especially when the Climbing Gauntlets are equipped.

- **Dodging and Sprinting**: Holding the sprint button consumes stamina but lets you evade or reposition quickly. Double-tap in any direction to perform a dodge roll, crucial for avoiding enemy attacks or environmental hazards.

Interaction and Environmental Navigation

The game encourages immersive exploration by making the world feel interactive and alive.

- **Contextual Interact Button**: One multi-purpose key allows you to talk to NPCs, open chests, inspect artifacts, read scrolls, or activate puzzles—depending on your proximity and what's available.

- **Ledge Grabs and Wall Hangs**: If you're near a climbable ledge, your character will automatically reach for it. Holding the interact button lets you hang on or pull yourself up.

- **Swimming and Diving**: When near water, you can wade, swim, or dive to reach underwater ruins, collect rare herbs, or avoid enemies. Diving consumes a breath meter that must be monitored.

- **Fast Travel Stones**: Once discovered, you can use Waystones to instantly travel between major locations. These are unlocked after completing introductory quests in each region.

HUD and Interface Elements

The interface is sleek, minimal, and customizable, designed to provide essential information without overwhelming the player.

- **Health and Stamina Bars**: Located in the upper-left corner. Stamina is consumed during running, dodging, or heavy attacks and regenerates over time.

- **Spirit Bond Gauge**: This special meter tracks your connection with Waqwaq spirits, which affects magical abilities and can unlock special combat effects or dialogue options.

- **Mini-map and Compass**: Always visible in Adventure Mode, showing nearby points of interest, quest markers, and hidden lore sites. Can be toggled off in Hardcore or Immersive Modes.

- **Quick Menu Wheel**: Pressing and holding a hotkey brings up a radial menu to access potions, gear sets, or magic without pausing the game.

Menus and Inventory Navigation

The pause menu is organized into several key sections, making inventory and progression management simple:

- **Inventory**: Organizes your gear, materials, and key items. Items are sortable by type, rarity, or usage.

- **Abilities**: A dedicated skill menu shows your unlocked powers, their upgrade trees, and the spirit influences attached to each.

- **Journal**: Contains quest logs, discovered lore, and character dialogue summaries.

- **Map and Objectives**: Displays a detailed regional map, fast travel options, and your active questlines.

- **Settings**: Customize your UI, accessibility options, control layout, audio balance, and display preferences from here.

Tips for New Players

- **Use the Spirit Pulse**: Holding down the Spirit Sense button reveals nearby interactables, hidden paths, and enemy weak points—an essential tool for new adventurers.

- **Practice Dodging Early**: Timing dodges will be critical against stronger enemies, especially in corrupted zones where damage can stack rapidly.

- **Save Often**: While the game autosaves regularly, manual saving at Waqwaq Shrines is highly recommended before entering high-risk areas or major story segments.

2.2 Combat System Explained

Combat in *Bahamut and the Waqwaq Tree* is a rich and tactical experience that combines fluid real-time action with deep strategic planning. Whether you're engaging in a one-on-one duel with a spirit-bound knight or facing swarms of corrupted creatures, the combat system adapts to your choices, loadouts, and playstyle. This section breaks down the core elements of combat, from weapon combos to spirit magic, and how to effectively combine them in battle.

Core Combat Mechanics

Combat is real-time, fast-paced, and reactive. It emphasizes positioning, timing, and synergy between physical and magical abilities.

- **Light and Heavy Attacks**: Each weapon type has unique combos for light (quick) and heavy (charged) attacks. Mixing them creates chained moves that can stagger enemies or break shields.

- **Dodging and Parrying**: Timing a dodge just before an enemy attack initiates a "Perfect Dodge," which slows time briefly and opens up a counter window. Parrying, when timed correctly, reflects damage and leaves the enemy vulnerable.

- **Target Lock-On**: Use the lock-on function to focus on a single target, which is especially useful during boss fights or crowded enemy encounters. Locking on also helps trigger specific abilities that require precise positioning.

Weapon Styles and Combo Variations

The game supports multiple weapon archetypes, each with its own rhythm and ideal use cases:

- **One-Handed Swords**: Balanced and beginner-friendly, allowing for quick combos and mobility.

- **Greatswords and Hammers**: High damage with slow wind-up. Best used against armored enemies or in crowd control situations.

- **Daggers and Dual Blades**: Emphasize speed and critical hits. Excellent for stealth kills and evasion-heavy builds.

- **Staves and Spirit Weapons**: Amplify magic abilities while offering mid-range combat effectiveness.

- **Bows and Chakrams**: Ranged options for kiting enemies and exploiting elemental weaknesses from afar.

Each weapon type can be augmented with elemental enchantments or spirit effects to enhance utility in different situations.

Magic and Spirit Abilities

Magic in *Bahamut and the Waqwaq Tree* is not just flashy—it's strategic, environmentally reactive, and deeply integrated with the lore.

- **Spirit Binding**: Players bond with spirits found throughout the world, which grant unique magical abilities based on their domain (e.g., fire, wind, decay, time).

- **Spellcasting System**: Spells are mapped to shortcuts and use a regenerating mana pool called "Waqwaq Essence." Elemental synergies—like casting wind before fire to create a firestorm—add tactical depth.

- **Ritual Casts and Channeling**: Powerful "Ritual Spells" can be cast with channel time and animation, often requiring you to remain stationary and vulnerable for a few seconds. These offer massive payoffs when used correctly.

Magic is not just for offense—certain spells create barriers, slow time, heal allies, or manipulate terrain.

Spirit Gauge and Ultimate Abilities

As you engage in combat and use spirit-infused skills, you charge your **Spirit Gauge**, which can be unleashed in devastating ways:

- **Guardian Forms**: Temporarily transform your character using the power of a bonded spirit, dramatically boosting your stats and altering your abilities.

- **Ultimate Attacks**: Each class or build has a unique ultimate, such as summoning an ethereal dragon, freezing time, or calling down divine judgment.

- **Synergy Finishers**: When fighting in co-op, players can coordinate their Spirit Gauges for devastating combination attacks that vary depending on their elemental affinities.

Enemy Behavior and AI Adaptation

Enemies in the game are not static—they adapt to your fighting style and require you to constantly evolve your tactics.

- **Pattern Recognition**: Bosses and elite foes will begin to recognize and counter repeated strategies.

- **Pack Tactics**: Enemy groups use flanking, baiting, and ambush mechanics, forcing you to control the battlefield.

- **Environmental Awareness**: Certain enemies react to terrain—forest beasts may use cover, while corrupted knights disrupt your footing on unstable platforms.

Understanding enemy behavior is crucial to surviving higher difficulties, particularly in Elder Trial Mode.

Combat Tips and Advanced Techniques

- **Use the Environment**: Lure enemies into hazardous areas like bramble traps or magical anomalies. Water conducts lightning; fire spreads in dry grass.

- **Interrupting Spells**: Heavy attacks and certain spells can interrupt enemy channeling animations. This is key to stopping deadly attacks before they begin.

- **Positioning Matters**: Flanking enemies or attacking from above gives critical strike bonuses. Some abilities can only be used from specific angles or positions.

- **Combo Canceling**: Skilled players can cancel out of certain animations (such as dodges or spellcasts) into others, allowing fluid chaining of attacks and evasions.

2.3 Exploration and Environmental Interaction

Exploration in *Bahamut and the Waqwaq Tree* is an immersive and rewarding experience that goes far beyond just moving from point A to point B. The game's world, Samar, is richly layered with ancient mysteries, interactive environments, and dynamic events that reward curious players. Traversing the varied biomes—from skybound isles to corrupted roots of the Waqwaq Tree—requires an understanding of both physical navigation and magical interaction with the environment.

Dynamic World Layout and Zones

The world of Samar is semi-open and interconnected, built around a hub-and-spoke model where zones open progressively as you complete quests and gain new abilities.

- **Biome Diversity**: Each major region is unique—Verdant Groves are lush and maze-like, the Ashen Plains are scorched and haunted by wind spirits, while the Canopy Labyrinth is a vertical jungle-city perched in the Waqwaq's branches.

- **Transition Zones**: Instead of hard loading screens, regions flow naturally into one another through caves, tree tunnels, or magic gates.

- **World Events**: Certain areas shift based on time of day, corruption level, or world-state (e.g., Waqwaq Blooming Season), revealing new paths or hazards.

The game encourages revisiting earlier areas with new abilities to uncover hidden secrets or alternate paths.

Environmental Puzzles and Spirit-Based Mechanics

Exploration isn't just about movement—it's about engaging with the environment using logic, magic, and timing.

- **Spirit Pulse**: A key mechanic that reveals hidden objects, weak walls, or spectral pathways. It also interacts with ancient glyphs and totems scattered across the world.

- **Elemental Interactions**: Use spirit magic to manipulate the environment. Fire can burn thorns, wind can push platforms, ice can freeze water to create bridges, and decay can age wooden barriers into dust.

- **Waqwaq Echoes**: Magical memories embedded in certain objects. Activating them replays spectral scenes from the past, offering clues to puzzles or unlocking new abilities if enough are collected.

- **Rune Locks and Nature Seals**: These require you to complete environmental challenges, such as aligning ancient symbols or solving movement-based puzzles, to unlock powerful artifacts or shortcut routes.

Exploration rewards thoughtfulness, observation, and experimentation.

Climbing, Swimming, and Traversal Tools

To aid in vertical and horizontal exploration, you'll acquire tools that expand your movement capabilities:

- **Climbing Gauntlets**: Allow vertical scaling of certain surfaces and clinging to overhangs.

- **Spirit Glider**: A magical leaf-glider powered by wind spirits that enables you to float across canyons or reach distant cliffs.

- **Rootwalker Boots**: Grants wall-running and double-jumping capabilities when near plant-based surfaces.

- **Breath of the Deep**: A spirit enhancement that lets you dive and explore underwater ruins without running out of air.

These tools are unlocked through progression or hidden quests, each adding a new layer of depth to how you interact with the environment.

Interactive NPCs, Side Quests, and Lore Points

Exploration is also narrative-driven. Talking to NPCs, examining landmarks, and investigating ruins can unravel deeper stories and worldbuilding.

- **Wandering Lorekeepers**: These characters travel between regions and provide historical background, clues to hidden locations, and even rare spell scrolls.

- **Cursed Shrines and Spirit Wells**: Optional challenge areas that test your combat, navigation, or puzzle-solving skills. Completing them often provides powerful rewards and rare collectibles.

- **Faction Outposts**: Throughout Samar, you'll encounter various factions—some friendly, others hostile. Aligning with or influencing these groups can open new questlines, vendors, or even entire regions.

- **Environmental Storytelling**: From skeletal remains locked in eternal battle to murals that change after key story events, the world tells its story visually for observant players.

NPC interaction also triggers dynamic world responses, such as changing weather patterns or corruption levels, making your choices feel tangible.

2.4 Managing Resources and Inventory

Efficient resource and inventory management is key to survival and success in *Bahamut and the Waqwaq Tree*. With a diverse array of items—ranging from consumables and crafting materials to rare spirit relics and gear upgrades—the game encourages careful planning and organization. Whether you're preparing for a boss fight, crafting potions, or optimizing your loadout for exploration, this section explains how to manage your inventory effectively, maximize your carry capacity, and make the most of your resources.

Inventory System Overview

The inventory in *Bahamut and the Waqwaq Tree* is broken down into several well-organized categories, each with distinct limits and filters for easy access:

- **Gear**: Weapons, armor sets, accessories, and spirit-bound items. Gear can be equipped, upgraded, or stored in your spirit locker.

- **Consumables**: Healing potions, spirit flasks, food buffs, and one-use magical tools.

- **Crafting Materials**: Herbs, ores, monster drops, elemental dust, and essence shards used in alchemy and smithing.

- **Quest Items**: Key story objects, maps, and tokens required to progress narrative arcs or open sealed pathways.

- **Relics and Collectibles**: Optional items that reveal lore, enhance abilities, or unlock achievements.

The game provides automatic sorting options (by rarity, weight, or type), quick-use slots, and lockable favorites to keep vital items accessible.

Resource Types and Their Usage

There are several core resource types players must monitor and utilize:

- **Goldleaf**: The game's primary currency used for trading, repairing gear, and fast travel costs.

- **Spirit Essence**: Collected from defeated enemies or harvested from shrines, it fuels magic upgrades and certain high-tier abilities.

- **Crafting Components**: Gathered from the environment or enemies. They're categorized by element (e.g., Flamebud, Glimmer Ore, Murkroot) and are essential for creating potions, gear, and enchantments.

- **Stamina and Mana**: Regenerating resources that govern combat and spell use. Managing these during long dungeon runs is crucial.

- **Encumbrance Level**: Your character has a weight threshold that affects dodge speed and stamina regeneration. Exceeding it can lead to penalties in movement and combat fluidity.

Balancing between carrying useful gear and staying agile is part of the strategy.

Crafting, Upgrading, and Item Fusion

The game features robust crafting and upgrading systems tied to exploration and resource gathering:

- **Potion Brewing**: At alchemy tables, mix herbs and spirit dust to create health elixirs, resistance potions, or elemental oils for weapons.

- **Weapon and Armor Enhancement**: Blacksmiths and spirit forges let you improve base stats or add sockets for spirit glyphs.

- **Rune Fusion**: Combine low-tier relics and glyphs to unlock powerful abilities or passive buffs.

- **Customization**: Certain rare materials allow you to modify the appearance of gear without affecting stats—a cosmetic-only system that caters to personal flair.

Crafting recipes are unlocked via exploration, side quests, or hidden scrolls found throughout Samar.

Storage and Spirit Locker System

As you accumulate gear and materials, managing storage becomes essential:

- **Spirit Locker**: Your personal storage chest accessible from Waqwaq Shrines and major settlements. Items stored here are safe and weightless.

- **Quick-Slot Loadouts**: Create preset builds that include weapons, armor, spells, and potions. Great for switching from exploration to combat or stealth-focused approaches.

- **Auto-Stash and Cleanup**: At any save point, you can choose to automatically store surplus crafting components or duplicate gear to streamline inventory.

Inventory space can be expanded through quest rewards, merchant upgrades, or discovering hidden packs scattered across the world.

Tips for Efficient Resource Management

- **Always Combine Before Selling**: Fused relics and crafted potions often sell for more than their base materials.

- **Scout Before You Craft**: Some items may be better saved for story progression puzzles or rare quests rather than consumed early on.

- **Use Markers**: Tag gear you plan to sell, upgrade, or store to avoid accidentally discarding valuable items.

- **Recycle Unneeded Gear**: Many unused weapons and armor can be broken down into crafting materials at specific forges, reducing waste and freeing space.

Chapter 3. Character Classes and Roles

3.1 Character Overview and Specializations

In *Bahamut and the Waqwaq Tree*, players can choose from a variety of character archetypes, each with distinct strengths, abilities, and affinities with spirit magic. Rather than locking players into a single class, the game promotes flexible progression and cross-specialization. However, each character begins their journey by selecting a base role that determines their early abilities and combat style.

Core Class Archetypes:

- **Warden of Flame** – A balanced melee-magic hybrid that channels fire spirits to enhance weapons and unleash AoE attacks.

- **Windblade Nomad** – A fast and agile fighter who excels in mobility, critical hits, and wind-based ranged abilities.

- **Stonecaller Sentinel** – A durable tank-like role, bonded with earth spirits, capable of absorbing damage and manipulating terrain.

- **Mistweaver Seer** – A spellcaster focused on support and control, using mist and water-based spells to heal allies or disorient enemies.

- **Hollow Dancer** – A stealthy rogue who communes with shadow spirits, excelling in evasion, traps, and ambushes.

Each role provides a different entry point into combat and exploration while allowing gradual evolution into hybrid styles.

3.2 Strengths and Weaknesses of Each Role

Understanding the advantages and trade-offs of each class role helps you adapt your strategy for different missions, enemies, and environments.

Warden of Flame

- *Strengths*: Balanced stats, solid damage output, adaptable to solo or team play.

- *Weaknesses*: Jack-of-all-trades, master of none; lacks specialization in high defense or mobility.

Windblade Nomad

- *Strengths*: High mobility, excellent for hit-and-run tactics, strong critical hit potential.

- *Weaknesses*: Low durability, vulnerable to area-of-effect attacks and crowd control.

Stonecaller Sentinel

- *Strengths*: High defense and stamina, excels at protecting allies and controlling space.

- *Weaknesses*: Slow movement, limited ranged options, depends on close-range engagement.

Mistweaver Seer

- *Strengths*: Versatile support role, powerful area control spells, healing over time.

- *Weaknesses*: Fragile in direct combat, heavily reliant on positioning and mana.

Hollow Dancer

- *Strengths*: Stealth gameplay, trap setting, crowd manipulation through fear or confusion.

- *Weaknesses*: Difficult learning curve, less effective in direct confrontations or boss fights.

Each role shines in specific mission types and synergizes uniquely in co-op play or with summoned spirit allies.

3.3 Abilities and Skills for Different Playstyles

Each character class has its own skill tree with branching paths for specialization, allowing players to tailor their builds to offensive, defensive, or hybrid strategies. Here's how each class adapts to different playstyles:

Aggressive/Damage-Oriented Builds

- *Warden of Flame*: Flame Surge, Firechain Blade, Blazing Ward

- *Windblade Nomad*: Cyclone Step, Razor Gale, Wind Repeater

- *Hollow Dancer*: Shadow Ambush, Wraith Mark, Venom Dagger

Tank/Support-Oriented Builds

- *Stonecaller Sentinel*: Rooted Guard, Earthshatter, Living Wall

- *Mistweaver Seer*: Spirit Rejuvenation, Torrent Snare, Mist Veil

Balanced/Control Builds

- Focus on spirit-based crowd control, battlefield manipulation, and utility effects like stun, slow, or terrain hazard creation.

All characters eventually unlock access to **Spirit Crossroads**, which allows limited access to another class's skills—opening up hybrid builds like a Mistweaver with stealth skills or a Nomad with defensive buffs.

3.4 Customizing Your Character's Growth

Character growth in *Bahamut and the Waqwaq Tree* is dynamic and personalized, offering a multi-path system of development beyond traditional leveling. Growth is influenced by combat choices, spirit bonds, and player decisions.

Leveling System

- Experience points (XP) are earned from combat, exploration, and quests.

- Each level grants **Attribute Points** (for stats) and **Spirit Points** (for unlocking new abilities).

Attribute Stats:

- **Vigor** – Affects health, resistance to corruption.

- **Agility** – Enhances dodge speed, crit chance, movement.

- **Focus** – Boosts spell power, essence regeneration.

- **Fortitude** – Increases armor, stagger resistance.

- **Resonance** – Determines bond strength with spirits and spirit ability power.

Spirit Bond Evolution

- The deeper your bond with a spirit, the more powerful its abilities become.

- Spirit paths can branch into unique evolutions (e.g., Fire → Infernal → Solar).

- Your choices during spirit trials influence the outcome of these evolutions.

Gear Scaling and Synergy

- Certain gear pieces offer bonuses when aligned with your class archetype or spirit bond.

- Equip sets that synergize with your current playstyle—light armor for stealth, runed robes for casters, or heavy barkplate for Sentinels.

Customization is further enhanced by narrative choices, faction alignment, and hidden relics that alter passive abilities. No two characters need grow the same way, allowing for deep replayability and experimentation.

Chapter 4. Weapons and Equipment

4.1 Types of Weapons and Their Functions

In *Bahamut and the Waqwaq Tree*, weapon choice greatly influences your combat approach, elemental affinity, and synergy with spirit abilities. Weapons are not only tools of offense—they often carry special passive traits, spirit slots, or environmental interactions that enhance their utility in exploration and puzzles.

Main Weapon Categories:

- **Blades (Swords, Scimitars, Sabers)**
  Fast and versatile, ideal for balanced play. Blades often carry elemental enchantments like fire or wind.

- **Polearms (Spears, Glaives, Staff-lances)**
  Offer extended reach and sweeping attacks. Effective against multiple enemies and airborne targets.

- **Great Weapons (Greatswords, Hammers, Battleaxes)**
  Slow but devastating. High stagger power and excellent for breaking enemy shields or armor.

- **Ranged Weapons (Spirit Bows, Chakrams, Blowpipes)**
  Allow you to fight from a distance. Many ranged weapons use spirit-infused ammo with unique effects like poison or sleep.

- **Spirit Channelers (Tomes, Spirit Orbs, Totems)**
  Focused on spellcasting and support. They enhance spirit
  affinity and amplify magical attacks or summons.

Each weapon category offers branching specializations—some
unlock through progression, others are tied to specific factions or
spirit bonds.

4.2 Armor and Defensive Gear

Armor sets in *Bahamut and the Waqwaq Tree* do more than protect.
They reflect your chosen path, boost specific stats, and synergize
with your spirit bond. Armor also comes in three main types:

Armor Types:

- **Light Armor**
  High agility and stamina recovery. Perfect for stealth or
  mobility-focused builds. Includes items like Spiritweave
  Robes and Echocloth Garb.

- **Medium Armor**
  Balanced defense and mobility. Great for hybrid builds or
  players who want both speed and survivability. Examples:
  Wyrmbark Leather, Skyguard Mantle.

- **Heavy Armor**
  High defense and stagger resistance. Ideal for tanks and
  frontline fighters. Often limits evasion but offers superior
  resistance to corruption or elemental damage. Includes
  Barkplate Greaves and Obsidian Shellmail.

Defensive Accessories:

- **Amulets and Rings**: Provide resistances, passive effects like mana regen, or spirit bond enhancements.

- **Wards and Totems**: Equipable defensive tools that can block spells or reduce cooldowns.

Armor sets sometimes grant **set bonuses** when worn together—such as reduced mana cost, enhanced spirit burst, or immunity to certain status effects.

4.3 Item Crafting and Upgrades

Crafting is a vital part of equipment management and customization. As you explore Samar, you'll collect rare materials, blueprints, and unlock forges that let you strengthen or transform your gear.

Crafting Components:

- **Elemental Ores**: Firesteel, Glimmershard, Tempest Quartz. Used for forging and enchantments.

- **Organic Materials**: Thornhide, Shadewool, Heartvine. Used in light armor and accessory crafting.

- **Essence Crystals**: Rare drops that fuel enchantments and spirit weapon evolutions.

Upgrade Systems:

- **Weapon Forging**: Increases base damage, unlocks combo extensions, and spirit glyph slots.

- **Armor Enhancement**: Boosts resistance stats, adds passive buffs, and reduces weight.

- **Infusion Runes**: Attach to weapons or armor to add effects like poison, shock, or health regeneration.

Spirit Imbuement: Legendary gear can bond with your primary spirit, evolving their powers. For example, a Windblade bonded with the Stormwhisper Spirit may unlock chain lightning effects.

Blueprints and crafting stations are scattered across the world or granted by NPCs. Some advanced gear requires solving puzzles, defeating mini-bosses, or completing faction quests to obtain.

4.4 Managing Your Equipment for Success

Having powerful gear is only part of the equation—knowing when and how to use it is what makes you unstoppable.

Loadout Management:

- **Multiple Weapon Sets**: Swap between two equipped weapons mid-combat. Useful for adapting to enemy resistances or switching between melee and ranged.

- **Elemental Preparation**: Bring gear that counters the enemy's elemental affinity (e.g., fire armor vs. ice bosses).

- **Quick-Slot Items**: Assign healing items, bombs, or spell-scrolls for instant access during combat.

Encumbrance and Weight Management:

- Heavy equipment slows your dodge, drains stamina faster, and may reduce spirit channeling speed.

- Equip accessories or enchantments that reduce gear weight or increase carry capacity to balance defense with agility.

Gear Synergy with Spirit Abilities:

- Certain weapons grant cooldown reductions or enhanced effects for specific spirits.

- Optimize your build by aligning your gear with your spirit type—e.g., a Flameblade for a Fire Spirit or Earthbound Armor for a Stonecaller.

Maintenance and Repairs:

- Gear degrades over time, especially after difficult battles or corrupted zones.

- Visit Spirit Smiths or use portable repair kits to maintain optimal gear performance.

Smart equipment management means fewer unnecessary deaths, more efficient combat, and better synergy with your playstyle. Whether you're delving into deep roots or soaring through sky gardens, the right gear setup can turn any encounter in your favor.

Chapter 5. Strategies and Tips

5.1 Early Game Tips for Beginners

Getting started in *Bahamut and the Waqwaq Tree* can be overwhelming due to its richly layered mechanics and open-ended exploration. These beginner tips can help new players find their footing and make early progress smoother:

1. Focus on Exploration

- Take your time exploring each area. Hidden shrines, spirit trials, and lore fragments often provide major rewards like XP boosts, gear, and spirit upgrades.

- Look for visual clues: overgrown roots, glowing glyphs, and humming sounds often signal secrets or hidden passages.

2. Choose a Playstyle-Friendly Class

- If you're unsure, start with the Warden of Flame for a balanced experience.

- Avoid high-skill classes like Hollow Dancer early on unless you're experienced with stealth and counter-based gameplay.

3. Bond Early with a Spirit

- The first spirit you bond with shapes your gameplay significantly. Choose one that complements your class: Fire for offense, Earth for defense, Wind for speed, Water for healing/support.

- Visit spirit shrines regularly to enhance your bond and unlock new powers.

4. Complete Side Quests

- Early side quests often unlock permanent bonuses like expanded inventory slots, fast travel, or spirit evolution branches.

- NPCs may offer gear and lore that deepen your understanding of the game world.

5. Learn Enemy Patterns

- Dodging, parrying, and recognizing telegraphs are key to survival. Each enemy type has specific cues before attacking—study them early.

5.2 Combat Tactics and Boss Fight Strategies

Combat in *Bahamut and the Waqwaq Tree* rewards timing, preparation, and tactical awareness. Here are strategies for mastering regular encounters and boss battles:

General Combat Tips:

- Always lock on to enemies in narrow areas or boss rooms. This improves camera control and target focus.

- Use environmental elements like collapsing bridges, spike roots, and elemental zones to your advantage.

- Spirit abilities can stagger, slow, or confuse enemies—use them to create openings.

Boss Fight Strategy Framework:

- **Scout First**: Observe the boss's moves and attack phases before rushing in. Most bosses have at least two phases with unique patterns.

- **Elemental Countering**: If a boss uses frost magic, equip fire-resistant gear and bring fire-based weapons for damage boosts.

- **Use Spirit Summons**: Summoned spirits can distract the boss, provide healing, or amplify your damage output.

- **Prepare Loadouts**: Customize your weapon set, potion stock, and spirit abilities for each boss fight. Some may require high mobility, while others demand ranged focus.

Specific Boss Tactics:

- **Rootbound Guardian**: Stay mobile; its root traps can immobilize you.

- **Ashwhisper Matriarch**: Keep distance and avoid poison clouds. Use ranged spirit attacks.

- **Sky-Eater Serpent**: Aerial boss requiring vertical mobility and ranged weapons. Use updrafts and zipvine anchors.

5.3 Resource Management for Progression

Progressing smoothly requires smart use of your materials, gear, and currency. Mismanaging resources can leave you underpowered or stuck.

Essentials:

- **Goldleaf**: Save for crucial upgrades and rare item trades, rather than minor purchases early on.

- **Spirit Essence**: Prioritize unlocking core spirit abilities first, then secondary effects or passives.

- **Crafting Materials**: Don't waste rare materials on low-tier gear. Wait until you've unlocked a blacksmith capable of infusing spirit elements.

Upgrading Strategy:

- Focus on one or two main weapons, rather than spreading materials across many.

- Upgrade armor strategically—pick sets that complement your current build or resist the environment you're heading into.

Inventory Tips:

- Sell or dismantle duplicate or low-level gear to free space and earn materials.

- Use the Spirit Locker often to store crafting mats and legacy gear for future builds or hybrids.

Consumable Efficiency:

- Use potions wisely. Spirit Flasks recharge at shrines, but custom-brewed potions do not.

- Always keep at least one status-resist item and one AoE potion for emergencies.

5.4 Navigating the Dangerous Waqwaq Tree

The Waqwaq Tree is not just a setting—it's a living, shifting maze filled with traps, spirit corruption, and spatial illusions. Success here requires both skill and awareness.

Key Navigation Tools:

- **Echo Seeds**: Plant these at key intersections to track your progress or create fast-travel nodes.

- **Spirit Sight**: Use this ability to reveal hidden paths, enemy auras, or break illusions.

- **Zipvine Anchors**: Grappling points hidden in canopy zones that allow access to secret upper levels or shortcut routes.

Area-Specific Hazards:

- **Verdant Maw**: Rotting roots release toxic spores. Equip poison-resistant gear.

- **Twilight Hollow**: Illusory floors and ghost traps. Spirit Sight is essential.

- **Canopy Spires**: High-altitude platforming areas with strong winds. Use Wind spirit boosts to stabilize your jumps.

Enemy Ambush Patterns:

- Enemies in the Waqwaq Tree often hunt in packs and strike from multiple angles.

- Use the environment—drop ledges, explosive roots, and fog fields—for defensive positioning.

Tips for Safe Travel:

- Always travel with at least two escape tools: smokebombs, spirit dash, or teleportation scrolls.

- Mark your map. The tree shifts slightly between visits, and manual markers help you avoid getting lost.

Chapter 6. Walkthroughs for Missions and Levels

6.1 Main Story Mission Walkthrough

The main storyline of *Bahamut and the Waqwaq Tree* spans five acts, taking you from the Outskirts of Samar to the Heart of the Waqwaq Tree itself. Each act introduces new environments, mechanics, and escalating challenges.

Act I – Roots of Rebellion

- **Objective**: Escape the Spiritbound Mines and discover your bond.

- **Highlights**: Learn core mechanics, bond with your first spirit, fight your first elite mini-boss (Stone Maw Beast).

- **Tips**: Use Spirit Sight to find a hidden passage in the Emberroot Tunnels for a rare armor set.

Act II – Echoes of the Verdant Maw

- **Objective**: Seek the Wyrm Oracle and uncover the corruption.

- **Boss**: Rootbound Guardian – Use fire-based weapons to burn through its regenerative bark armor.

- **Tips**: Follow fireflies to hidden memory fragments that unlock lore-based upgrades.

Act III – The Skyward Canopy

- **Objective**: Reignite the Sky Lanterns and earn the favor of the Wind Court.

- **Mechanics Introduced**: Vertical traversal, grappling with Zipvine Anchors, aerial combat.

- **Tips**: Equip gear that reduces fall damage; use wind spirits for improved mobility.

Act IV – Hollowheart Depths

- **Objective**: Recover the Cradle Relic and resist spirit corruption.

- **Environment**: Dark, claustrophobic tunnels, traps, and hallucinations.

- **Tips**: Equip a torch weapon or spirit with light aura to counter the dark zone debuffs.

Act V – The Heart of the Waqwaq Tree

- **Objective**: Face Bahamut's inner trial and restore balance to the Tree.

- **Final Boss**: The Bound Bahamut – a multi-phase spirit-beast corrupted by void energy.

- **Tips**: Maximize your spirit bond and prepare for a test of everything you've learned—mobility, timing, and resource conservation.

6.2 Side Quests and Optional Objectives

Side quests are not just filler—they often yield rare gear, unique spirits, and vital lore insights. Here are key side quests worth your time:

"The Lost Flamekeeper" (Act I)

- **Location**: Emberroot Caverns.

- **Reward**: Emberbrand Torch (a light-source weapon with bonus damage vs corrupted foes).

- **Tip**: Look for soot trails and glowing moss to find the hidden tomb.

"Windswept Trials" (Act III)

- **Location**: Skyward Canopy.

- **Objective**: Complete three aerial traversal puzzles.

- **Reward**: Windwalker Sigil (enhances jump height and air control).

"Song of the Hollow Ones" (Act IV)

- **Location**: Hollowheart Depths.

- **Reward**: Passive spirit ability "Echo Rebound" (reflects projectiles when below 25% HP).

- **Tip**: Use a Seer's Cloak to understand ghost whispers and complete the musical puzzle.

Faction Objectives

- Join one of the three major factions (Flamebound, Skyscribes, Verdant Pact) for exclusive quests, gear, and endgame story branches.

6.3 Strategies for Surviving the Waqwaq Tree's Challenges

The Waqwaq Tree is a labyrinthine biome of bioluminescent canopies, root mazes, shifting paths, and corrupted zones. Here's how to survive:

1. Map Awareness

- The in-game map is unreliable in deep Waqwaq zones. Use Echo Seeds to mark your path and spirit markers to track safe zones.

2. Gear Up for Terrain

- Equip traversal gear like climbing claws, glider cloaks, or anti-root boots based on the region.

- Elemental hazards vary per biome—flame protection in Hollowroots, anti-venom for Verdant Maw.

3. Watch for Ambush Patterns

- Tree creatures often ambush from ceilings or blend into the bark. Use Spirit Sight periodically.

- Place warning traps behind you when resting in high-alert areas.

4. Avoid Nightfall Unprepared

- The Tree shifts during nighttime, with stronger corrupted enemies and fewer escape routes.

- Use Twilight Flasks or set up Spirit Beacons to survive until dawn.

6.4 Boss Fights and How to Conquer Them

Each boss in *Bahamut and the Waqwaq Tree* has unique mechanics and thematic ties to their region. Below are general strategies and some boss-specific advice:

General Boss Tips:

- Learn patterns: Most bosses follow a three-pattern cycle—observe before attacking.

- Break stamina: Many bosses have hidden stamina bars. Parrying or dodging at the right time can expose them to high-damage phases.

- Spirit synergy: Pick a spirit with debuffs, like Slumber Mist or Chainlight, to weaken bosses or delay their phases.

Key Bosses:

Rootbound Guardian (Act II)

- *Mechanics*: Massive AoE roots and regeneration.

- *Strategy*: Use fire weapons to cauterize wounds and disable healing phase.

Ashwhisper Matriarch (Optional - Act III)

- *Mechanics*: Poison fields, summoned ash minions.

- *Strategy*: Equip gear with poison resistance; defeat minions quickly or they'll explode.

The Wailing Hollow (Act IV)

- *Mechanics*: Psychological attacks, dark zones, mirror clones.

- *Strategy*: Use light-based spirit to weaken illusions; avoid attacking mirror clones or suffer rebound damage.

Bound Bahamut (Final Boss)

- *Mechanics*: Multi-phase, hybrid melee/spell/spirit boss. Uses corrupted versions of your own abilities.

- *Strategy*: Prepare for a long fight—rotate cooldowns, conserve potions, and exploit its stagger windows in Phase 2.

Chapter 7. Secrets and Collectibles

7.1 Hidden Areas and Secret Locations

Throughout *Bahamut and the Waqwaq Tree*, there are numerous hidden areas and secret locations that reward exploration, curiosity, and puzzle-solving. Some of these areas hold powerful gear, rare crafting materials, and deep lore, while others are simply fun to uncover.

1. Hidden Shrines

- **Location**: These shrines are scattered throughout the Waqwaq Tree, often tucked into hard-to-reach places or shrouded by natural obstacles.

- **Rewards**: Unlock rare spirit bonds, enhanced abilities, and permanent stat boosts.

- **Tip**: Look for abnormal flora—shiny roots, unusual flowers, or glowing bark—that marks the presence of these shrines.

2. The Spirit Pools

- **Location**: Deep within the Verdant Maw or in isolated Canopy Spires.

- **Description**: These pools are places of great power. By completing a specific puzzle or defeating a nearby spirit guardian, you can gain access to them.

- **Reward**: Increased spirit bond capacity, extra essence, or unique spirit abilities.

- **Tip**: Use Spirit Sight to spot hidden pool entrances that may otherwise be camouflaged.

3. The Corrupted Hollow

- **Location**: An optional, hidden zone in the Hollowheart Depths.

- **Challenges**: Enemies are stronger and there's a dangerous corruption aura that slowly drains health.

- **Reward**: Legendary crafting materials, a special weapon blueprint, and the "Heart of the Waqwaq" relic.

- **Tip**: Only attempt this area after obtaining high-level resistance gear and a full inventory of healing items.

4. The Secret Garden of Bahamut

- **Location**: Near the base of the Waqwaq Tree, hidden behind illusions.

- **Rewards**: Discover a peaceful environment with treasure chests and unique enemies guarding Bahamut's long-lost artifacts.

- **Tip**: Trigger the illusion break by using Spirit Sight while performing a specific action (e.g., solving a nearby puzzle or speaking to a certain NPC).

7.2 Collectibles and Their Role in the Story

Collectibles serve a significant role in unraveling the deeper lore of *Bahamut and the Waqwaq Tree*. These items provide context to the history of the world, the spirits, and the Tree itself, enriching your understanding of the narrative.

1. Lore Fragments

- **Location**: Scattered throughout the game world in chests, secret alcoves, or hidden behind environmental puzzles.

- **Purpose**: Provide story snippets, background on the Waqwaq Tree's origin, and the rise of Bahamut.

- **Collection Bonus**: After collecting enough fragments, you unlock the "Keeper of Secrets" achievement, which grants the ability to see hidden lore in NPC dialogues.

2. Spirit Runes

- **Location**: Found in hidden shrines, often guarded by mini-bosses or rare enemies.

- **Purpose**: Enhance the abilities of the spirits you bond with. Runes add new combat abilities or passives for spirits, making them more powerful.

- **Collection Bonus**: Unlocks new spirit abilities and traits when all runes are collected, and unlocks the Spirit Mastery trait.

3. Ancient Relics

- **Location**: Rarely found, these relics are linked to significant historical events, hidden in the deepest, most dangerous zones of the Tree.

- **Purpose**: Each relic reveals a part of Bahamut's ancient past, showing his corruption and the true power of the Waqwaq Tree.

- **Collection Bonus**: Completing the relic collection grants you a special ability—"Memory of the Lost," which increases your damage output after defeating a boss or mini-boss.

7.3 Easter Eggs and Fun Discoveries

Bahamut and the Waqwaq Tree is full of delightful Easter eggs that reference other games, pop culture, and hidden homages to the developers' favorite things. These surprises add a layer of charm to the game.

1. Hidden Developer Rooms

- **Location**: Rarely accessed, but within specific caves or between areas that don't seem to have an entrance.

- **Description**: A fun homage to the developers, featuring quirky NPCs, developer art, and humorous dialogue.

- **Tip**: Try interacting with anything unusual in the environment—strange patterns of mushrooms, odd statues, or oddly placed doors that lead to these rooms.

2. Legendary Creature Encounter

- **Location**: The Wind-Swept Fields area near the highest peak in the Skyward Canopy.

- **Creature**: A flying creature named "Mischief of the Winds," that only appears after solving an ancient riddle.

- **Reward**: A rare cosmetic item (wind-touched wings) and the "Wind-Speaker" title.

3. The Bizarre Butterfly

- **Location**: Throughout the Waqwaq Tree, in areas with dense foliage or in light-filtered forests.

- **Trigger**: These butterflies appear when you are near rare materials or the spirit bond is at its peak.

- **Reward**: Following it will lead to a hidden location containing a powerful artifact or an elemental upgrade.

4. Secret NPC Encounters

- **Location**: Randomly appearing in hidden nooks or corners of the map.

- **Characters**: NPCs with quirky personalities who share odd stories, sell unique trinkets, or offer rare side quests.

- **Reward**: Rare items, unique spirits, or "favors" that assist in battle.

7.4 Unlockable Content and Special Rewards

Unlockable content is a major motivator for many players, and *Bahamut and the Waqwaq Tree* does not disappoint. From secret character skins to unique abilities, there's plenty to unlock.

1. Alternate Costumes and Skins

- **How to Unlock**: Many character skins, such as the "Fury of the Tree" outfit or "Spirit-Worn Armor," are unlocked after completing secret challenges or by collecting all lore fragments.

- **Bonus**: These skins not only change your appearance but also provide minor stat boosts.

2. New Game+ Mode

- **How to Unlock**: Complete the main story, then return to the game's title screen and choose the "Start New Game+" option.

- **Reward**: This mode allows you to carry over your gear, spirit bonds, and some abilities, but it increases the difficulty of enemies, adds additional challenges, and offers exclusive New Game+ content.

3. Legendary Spirit Summons

- **How to Unlock**: After gathering all Spirit Runes and relics, you unlock the ability to summon Legendary Spirits such as "Phoenix of the Skies" or "Elder Tree's Guardian."

- **Effect**: These spirits are more powerful than regular spirits and offer unique powers that drastically alter combat, such as massive AoE attacks or healing rain.

4. Secret Endings

- **How to Unlock**: Fulfill a set of specific, obscure conditions, such as choosing certain dialogue options, helping hidden NPCs, and collecting every collectible in the game.

- **Reward**: Unlocks the secret ending cutscene, revealing the true fate of Bahamut and the Waqwaq Tree, and granting a new game mechanic or spirit ability.

Chapter 8. Achievements and Trophies

8.1 Overview of Achievements and Trophies

In *Bahamut and the Waqwaq Tree*, achievements and trophies serve as milestones to showcase a player's accomplishments throughout the game. These rewards often encourage players to explore every corner of the game world, test their skills in combat, and master complex game mechanics.

Types of Achievements:

- **Story-based Achievements**: These are awarded as you progress through the main storyline. Completing key plot milestones will earn you these.

- **Combat and Gameplay Achievements**: Earned by defeating powerful bosses, mastering combat techniques, or completing specific challenges in combat.

- **Exploration Achievements**: Awarded for discovering secret areas, hidden collectibles, and completing side quests.

- **Special Challenges**: Unlock trophies for completing specific, difficult tasks or for achieving unique feats under specific conditions.

Trophy Categories:

- **Bronze**: Earned for completing basic tasks and early game milestones.

- **Silver**: Rewarded for more challenging objectives or significant accomplishments.

- **Gold**: The highest-level achievements, typically reserved for difficult, endgame feats.

- **Platinum**: Awarded for completing the entire list of achievements, often for 100% game completion.

8.2 Tips for Earning All Achievements

While earning every achievement may seem daunting, following these tips will help you efficiently tackle the tasks and unlock all the rewards.

1. Prioritize the Story-Driven Achievements

- **Focus on main plot progression** first, as it will naturally unlock many of the basic achievements related to combat, exploration, and story milestones.

- Achievements like "Warden of Flame" (defeat the first story boss) and "Echoes of the Past" (unlock a major lore section) will unlock as you progress through the game.

2. Map Out Exploration Goals Early

- Make sure to fully explore each area to unlock exploration-based achievements. Look for hidden shrines, secret locations, and paths that lead to collectible items.

- Use the in-game map, but also keep an eye out for visual clues such as peculiar markings on trees, strange natural formations, or glowing trails that suggest hidden paths.

3. Engage with Side Content

- Side quests and optional objectives offer not only rewards but also achievements. Completing these will unlock significant bonuses, as well as achievement milestones like "Devotee of the Tree" or "Master of Spirits."

- Completing faction-specific objectives is an excellent way to unlock a variety of trophies.

4. Use Spirit Bonds to Tackle Difficult Challenges

- Many combat and exploration-related achievements require you to enhance your spirits and use them strategically. Earning achievements like "Spirit Master" (max out a spirit's level) or "Summon Fury" (perform a specific spirit combo in combat) requires mastery of the spirit system.

- Make sure to bond with multiple spirits and experiment with combinations to unlock spirit-related trophies.

5. Time and Patience for Combat Achievements

- Many of the harder combat trophies, such as "Beast Slayer" (defeat 50 elite creatures) or "One With the Elements" (defeat bosses using only elemental attacks), require focused effort. Equip elemental weapons and perfect your combat timing to earn these trophies.

8.3 Missable Achievements and How to Get Them

Some achievements in *Bahamut and the Waqwaq Tree* are missable, meaning they can only be unlocked at certain points in the game, and if you skip a specific event or action, you may not be able to earn them on subsequent playthroughs. Here's a list of some important missable achievements and how to avoid missing them:

1. "Keeper of the Echoes" (Missable in Act I)

- **Description**: This achievement is earned by collecting the first Lore Fragment in the Emberroot Caverns.

- **How to Get It**: Be sure to explore every nook and cranny of the Emberroot Caverns during the early hours of the game. Once you progress beyond the caverns, you cannot go back to collect this fragment.

- **Tip**: Backtrack in the early areas before proceeding with the main quest to ensure you've collected all lore fragments.

2. "Blessing of the Old Gods" (Missable in Act II)

- **Description**: Earned by completing the "Wyrm Oracle's Trial" before defeating the Rootbound Guardian.

- **How to Get It**: After receiving the quest to speak with the Wyrm Oracle, make sure you complete this trial before tackling the Rootbound Guardian. If you defeat the Guardian first, the trial becomes unavailable.

- **Tip**: Check your quest log before entering the boss arena to ensure the trial is still active.

3. "Unseen Paths" (Missable in Act III)

- **Description**: Unlock by discovering a hidden area within the Skyward Canopy, accessible only after defeating the Sky-Eater Serpent.

- **How to Get It**: Once you defeat the Serpent, a hidden pathway becomes available. If you don't take it immediately, it's sealed off for the rest of the game.

- **Tip**: As soon as the serpent is defeated, explore the nearby area for a concealed entrance. Don't rush forward in the story.

4. "Flamebringer's Will" (Missable in Act V)

- **Description**: This trophy is unlocked by completing a series of flame-based trials in the Heart of the Waqwaq Tree.

- **How to Get It**: Be sure to activate all flame-based trials during your final journey through the Heart. Missing one trial will prevent you from unlocking this achievement.

- **Tip**: If you are nearing the final boss, backtrack through the area and double-check any areas you may have missed.

8.4 Special Achievements for Completionists

Completionists will find plenty of achievements to unlock, especially for those who aim to complete every side quest, collect every item, and master every mechanic. These achievements reward you for thorough exploration and dedication.

1. "Waqwaq Explorer" (Completionist Achievement)

- **Description**: Unlock this by discovering every hidden area and secret location in the game.

- **How to Get It**: Fully explore all zones and uncover every secret passage, shrine, and collectible hidden throughout the Waqwaq Tree.

- **Reward**: The achievement grants the "True Explorer" title and access to a unique travel speed bonus.

2. "Master of Spirits" (Completionist Achievement)

- **Description**: Earn this by maxing out the level of every spirit in the game.

- **How to Get It**: Dedicate time to bonding with all spirits, completing their individual spirit trials, and leveling them up to their maximum potential.

- **Reward**: Unlocks a special ability, "Essence of the Spirits," which boosts all combat stats when spirits are summoned.

3. "Waqwaq Herald" (Completionist Achievement)

- **Description**: This achievement is unlocked by completing every side quest and faction task.

- **How to Get It**: Ensure you take the time to complete all side content, including minor quests and optional objectives.

- **Reward**: Grants the "Herald of the Waqwaq" title and a special mount to aid in travel.

4. "The Eternal Flame" (Completionist Achievement)

- **Description**: Earned by collecting all flame-based relics scattered throughout the game.

- **How to Get It**: These relics are found in challenging, high-risk zones—usually requiring perfect traversal, combat, and puzzle-solving skills.

- **Reward**: Unlocks the Phoenix's Blessing passive, which gives you increased healing and stamina regeneration during combat.

Chapter 9. Advanced Techniques

9.1 Mastering Combat and Advanced Movement

Combat in *Bahamut and the Waqwaq Tree* can be incredibly dynamic and requires precise control, timing, and a deep understanding of the mechanics. To truly master the combat system and movement, you'll need to practice advanced techniques that enhance both your offensive and defensive capabilities.

1. Combos and Skill Chains

- **Mastering Combos**: Learn to chain different weapon attacks, spirit abilities, and elemental powers together for devastating combos. Certain weapons allow for multi-hit combos, while spirits provide unique buffs and attacks that can be woven into these chains.

- **Timing**: Advanced players will benefit from precise timing. Each weapon and spirit has specific windows where certain attacks deal higher damage or trigger additional effects. Mastering the rhythm of these attacks can maximize your damage output.

2. Perfect Dodging and Countering

- **Perfect Dodge**: Use the dodge mechanic to its fullest by timing your rolls to dodge enemy attacks just before impact. A well-timed dodge gives you a brief window to perform a counterattack or trigger a special ability.

- **Counterattack Skills**: Some characters and spirits allow for powerful counterattacks when you dodge at the right moment. Learn the timing for these to deal massive damage with minimal effort.

3. Environmental Interaction

- **Using the Environment to Your Advantage**: The world of *Bahamut and the Waqwaq Tree* is not only beautiful but also interactive. Advanced players can use their surroundings— such as boulders, trees, or structures—to deal with enemies. For example, luring enemies into tight spots where they can't dodge your attacks or triggering environmental hazards to damage groups of enemies can give you an edge.

- **Vertical Movement**: Mastering the use of vertical space is crucial, especially in areas like the Canopy Spires or Skyward Fields. Use aerial attacks, jumping off ledges, and dodging through narrow spaces to outmaneuver enemies.

4. Managing Multiple Targets

- **Area of Effect (AoE) Skills**: Master skills that target multiple enemies at once. This is particularly useful in larger fights or when faced with swarms of enemies. Learning to quickly switch between targets while keeping control of the battlefield is key to surviving tougher encounters.

- **Targeting and Lock-On**: Some enemies and bosses require precise targeting, and the lock-on system is essential. Learn how to quickly switch between targets and disable enemy projectiles or shield abilities for greater efficiency in combat.

9.2 Optimizing Your Build and Playstyle

Understanding and optimizing your character's build is essential for advancing through the tougher challenges in *Bahamut and the Waqwaq Tree*. Each playstyle has unique strengths and weaknesses, and refining your build to suit your preferred combat method will enhance your overall experience.

1. Understanding Stat Distribution

- **Focus on Core Stats**: Each character class benefits from specific stat increases. For instance, a warrior class may benefit from higher strength and defense, while a spellcaster will benefit from intelligence and magic power. Understand which stats are critical for your chosen role.

- **Balance vs. Specialization**: While balancing stats across various attributes is helpful in some situations, specialized builds (focusing on one or two key stats) can lead to powerful abilities and optimized performance. For example, focusing entirely on speed and evasion for a rogue build will allow you to avoid damage while dealing quick strikes.

2. Selecting the Right Spirits

- **Choosing the Right Spirit for Your Build**: Different spirits provide various benefits, from healing to elemental damage or tanking capabilities. If you're building a DPS (damage-per-second) character, focus on spirits that provide damage boosts or high damage abilities. For tank builds, select spirits that bolster your defense or provide support abilities.

- **Synergy Between Spirit Abilities and Weapon Skills**: Some spirits work better with specific weapon types. For instance, a heavy sword wielded by a spirit focused on brute force will deal massive damage with specific combo moves. Learn how to synergize your chosen spirit with your weapon.

3. Using Buffs and Debuffs

- **Maximizing Buffs**: Learn when to use buff abilities before heading into tougher battles. Certain spells or items can enhance your speed, damage resistance, or elemental power. Using these at the right moment can turn the tide of a fight.

- **Debuffing Enemies**: Some enemies have powerful abilities that can turn the fight in their favor. Use debuffing tactics, such as poison, freezing, or weakening effects, to mitigate their offensive power. Understanding enemy weaknesses is crucial in optimizing your approach.

4. Weapon and Armor Customization

- **Crafting and Upgrading**: Use crafting materials to enhance your weapons and armor to match your build. Increasing weapon durability and adding elemental effects can help you tackle specific types of enemies more effectively.

- **Elemental Resistance**: Tailor your armor to counteract environmental hazards or elemental damage from specific enemies. This can be key in surviving difficult areas like the Corrupted Hollow or the Heart of the Tree.

9.3 Speedrunning and Efficient Strategies

For players looking to complete the game quickly or optimize their time, speedrunning and efficient playthrough strategies are crucial. Mastering these techniques will allow you to enjoy the game in a whole new way.

1. Route Planning

- **Efficient Exploration**: In speedrunning, every second counts. Plan your route carefully, minimizing unnecessary backtracking. Stick to main objectives and avoid detours unless they are essential for unlocking required collectibles or resources.

- **Skip Non-Essential Battles**: Focus on only the necessary combat encounters, skipping fights that are not required to progress. Use stealth or strategic movement to avoid enemies when possible.

2. Utilizing Movement Techniques

- **Advanced Movement Glitches**: Some advanced players use glitches or exploit mechanics (like jumping over walls or skipping sections of the map) to reduce travel time. These require practice but can save significant time in a speedrun.

- **Fast Travel Mastery**: Use fast travel points effectively to skip long stretches of the map. Mastering the game's fast travel mechanics will reduce the need to travel on foot or on mounts, speeding up the overall pace.

3. Combat Skip Techniques

- **Interrupting Enemy Attacks**: Certain enemies can be skipped entirely by interrupting their attacks at the right moment or triggering certain events that bypass combat sequences. Learning how to trigger these events quickly can save a lot of time.

- **Boss Fights Strategy**: Speedrunners often focus on exploiting boss weaknesses to defeat them quickly. Use high-damage combos or elemental weaknesses to bring down bosses in record time. Familiarize yourself with each boss's attack patterns for the most efficient takedown.

4. Timed Challenges and Requirements

- **Minimizing Time Spent on Exploration**: Time-sensitive challenges (such as escaping areas or completing tasks within a limited window) require efficiency. Focus on upgrading speed and agility to finish these tasks in the shortest time possible.

- **Mastering Key Timed Events**: Some key events in the game are timed. Practice these events to avoid wasting time and reduce the overall length of your speedrun.

9.4 Customizing the Game's Difficulty for Advanced Players

Bahamut and the Waqwaq Tree offers a range of difficulty options to cater to all types of players. Advanced players may want to tailor their experience for the ultimate challenge.

1. Adjusting Combat Difficulty

- **Hard Mode**: Choose Hard Mode for more challenging enemies, tougher bosses, and limited resources. In this mode, you'll have to maximize your combat efficiency and resource management to survive.

- **Customizing Enemy Behavior**: Some areas allow you to adjust specific enemy behaviors, such as aggression, defense, or attack speed. Customize these options to fine-tune the challenge and create a unique experience.

2. Resource Management Adjustments

- **Scarcity Mode**: In this mode, resources such as health potions and crafting materials are extremely limited, forcing players to be strategic about what they use and when.

- **Limited Saves**: Some players prefer to add an extra layer of difficulty by limiting the number of save points available. This forces you to think carefully about when and where to save your progress.

3. Permadeath Mode

- **Extreme Challenge**: For the ultimate challenge, permadeath mode disables checkpoints and saves. If you die, you must restart the game from the beginning.

- **Survival Tactics**: This mode demands perfect combat techniques, resource management, and knowledge of the game's world and mechanics.

4. Tailoring Boss Fights

- **Adjust Boss Mechanics**: In some cases, you can alter boss difficulty by adding new phases or additional attacks, creating a truly challenging experience.

- **Boss Speed and Damage Buffs**: Increase the speed and damage of boss encounters for a heightened sense of urgency, pushing you to maximize your combat strategies.

Chapter 10. Additional Resources

10.1 Official Game Website and Forums

For all official information regarding *Bahamut and the Waqwaq Tree*, the official game website and forums are invaluable resources. Here, players can find updates, announcements, and a wealth of information directly from the developers.

1. Game Updates and Patch Notes

- **Stay Updated**: The official game website is the first place to look for important updates, including patch notes, bug fixes, and new content releases. These updates ensure that players stay informed about changes to the game's mechanics, new features, and fixes for any issues that may arise.

- **Changelog**: Detailed patch notes provide information about game balance adjustments, character updates, and bug fixes. Checking the changelog can help players stay ahead of the curve.

2. Developer Insights and Blogs

- **Behind-the-Scenes Content**: The official website often includes developer blogs, interviews, and behind-the-scenes videos. These insights can help players understand the creative process behind the game, the lore, and the worldbuilding of *Bahamut and the Waqwaq Tree.*

- **Development Roadmap**: Keep an eye on any upcoming expansions, DLCs, or planned content for the game. This resource gives players an idea of what to expect in future updates.

3. Official Forums for Community Interaction

- **Discuss Game Mechanics**: The official forums offer a space for players to discuss game strategies, share tips, and help each other with difficult sections of the game. It's also the place to report bugs or suggest features directly to the developers.

- **Community Feedback**: Forums are an excellent place for players to share their opinions and provide feedback on new features or gameplay elements. Developers may use this feedback to improve the game.

10.2 Community Resources and Fan Websites

The *Bahamut and the Waqwaq Tree* community is filled with passionate players who often create content, guides, and resources to help others progress. Fan-run websites and community platforms are excellent tools for expanding your experience with the game.

1. Game Wikis

- **Comprehensive Guides**: Many community-driven wikis provide detailed information on everything from lore and character backstories to step-by-step mission guides. These wikis are invaluable for those looking to complete the game 100% or find hidden secrets and collectibles.

- **Tips and Tricks**: Community wikis often have dedicated pages for tips, strategies, and optimizations that can make your journey easier.

2. YouTube Channels and Streams

- **Walkthroughs and Tutorials**: Many gamers create YouTube videos or Twitch streams that showcase their playthroughs, guides for specific bosses, or detailed explanations of combat mechanics. These resources can be especially helpful for visual learners.

- **Speedrunning Communities**: If you're interested in speedrunning, you can find plenty of content from the game's community. Speedrunners often provide their own tips and strategies to optimize gameplay for quick and efficient playthroughs.

3. Fan-Made Art and Storytelling

- **Creative Content**: Fans often produce incredible fan art, fan fiction, and other forms of creative content related to *Bahamut and the Waqwaq Tree*. These creations add to the game's world and can be a great way to appreciate the game from a different perspective.

- **Sharing Your Own Creations**: Whether it's drawing characters, designing new spirits, or writing fan fiction, the community is always welcoming of new content. Fans are encouraged to share their work through fan websites, social media, and online communities.

10.3 Modding Communities and Custom Content

If you're looking to further personalize your experience with *Bahamut and the Waqwaq Tree*, modding communities can be a great place to explore custom content, gameplay tweaks, and user-generated modifications.

1. Official Modding Support

- **Game Modding Tools**: Some games offer official modding tools or support, allowing players to create their own content, such as new weapons, characters, or entire levels. If *Bahamut and the Waqwaq Tree* offers such tools, they'll be found on the official website, enabling players to expand the game with user-generated content.

- **Modding Guidelines**: The game's modding community usually has specific guidelines and rules regarding what mods are acceptable. Make sure to follow these to ensure a smooth experience.

2. Community Mods and Custom Content

- **Mods for Improved Graphics and Audio**: Community mods often enhance the game's visual effects, add high-quality textures, or update character models for a more immersive experience.

- **Gameplay Mods**: Players can also find mods that tweak the game's mechanics, add new difficulty levels, alter combat styles, or introduce new features and systems to the gameplay. Mods can range from simple quality-of-life improvements to complete gameplay overhauls.

- **New Quests and Storylines**: Some mods introduce additional quests or alternate storylines. If you're looking for fresh content after completing the main game, mods can significantly extend your playthrough experience.

3. Modding Communities and Platforms

- **Steam Workshop**: If you play *Bahamut and the Waqwaq Tree* on Steam, the Steam Workshop may host mods created by the community. Here, you can easily browse, install, and manage mods to customize your game experience.

- **Nexus Mods**: Nexus Mods is another popular platform where you can find mods for the game. It offers a large variety of mods, including bug fixes, graphical enhancements, and custom gameplay changes.

- **Reddit and Modding Forums**: Subreddits and modding forums dedicated to the game are great places to find discussions about new mods, troubleshooting issues, and recommendations from the community.

10.4 Troubleshooting and Technical Support

If you encounter technical issues while playing *Bahamut and the Waqwaq Tree*, whether it's game crashes, performance problems, or bugs, there are several resources available to help you troubleshoot and get support.

1. Official Technical Support

- **Submitting Support Tickets**: If you're experiencing a bug or issue that's affecting gameplay, the official game website often has a support section where you can submit a ticket. Provide detailed information about the problem, such as what caused the issue and any error messages that appeared.

- **Contacting Customer Service**: Most games provide customer service contact details for troubleshooting. Reach out to the official support team for in-depth help with resolving any technical problems you're facing.

2. Troubleshooting Guides

- **Common Issues**: Look for official guides or FAQs on the website for common issues, such as installation problems, performance issues, or crashes. These guides may offer quick fixes or suggestions for resolving minor bugs.

- **Optimization Tips**: Some games may have performance issues on specific hardware setups. If you're facing frame rate drops or crashes, check for guides on optimizing your graphics settings for the best performance.

3. Community Troubleshooting

- **Community Solutions**: If you're facing a specific issue, the game's community forums or Reddit threads can be an excellent resource for troubleshooting. Many players share solutions to common problems that may not be officially documented.

- **Patch Workarounds**: If a particular bug is widespread, the community may create temporary workarounds or mods to resolve it until an official patch is released.

4. Updating Your Drivers and Software

- **Ensure Compatibility**: Make sure that your system's drivers, especially for your graphics card and operating system, are up to date. Often, performance issues and crashes are caused by outdated drivers or conflicting software.

- **Verify Game Files**: If you're playing on a platform like Steam, use the "Verify Integrity of Game Files" tool to check for missing or corrupted files. This can help resolve crashes or issues that may occur during gameplay.